Don't Go There
COLM KEEGAN

salmonpoetry

Published in 2012 by
Salmon Poetry
Cliffs of Moher, County Clare, Ireland
Website: www.salmonpoetry.com
Email: info@salmonpoetry.com

ISBN 978-1-908836-06-9

COVER PHOTOGRAPHY: *Erica Keegan*
COVER DESIGN: *Siobhán Hutson*

Salmon Poetry receives financial support from The Arts Council

'If you want to view paradise, simply look around and view it.'

LESLIE BRICUSSE

Acknowledgements

Acknowledgements are due to the following in which some of the poems from this collection were first published or broadcast:

The Poetry Bus: "Fridays"
Southword: "Ode to the Coalman"
County Lines: "Being Blown Backwards"
Night and Day: "Dear Dealer"
Caught in Amber, an anthology edited by Eileen Casey: "One Kick" and "Coats".

"Stony, Grey, Soiled", "Hazelnuts" and "Glowing Embers" were first published in *The Sunday Tribune* as entries into the Hennessy XO New Irish Writing Award.

"A Christmas Wish" was written for RTE Radio 1's *Arena* show and aired in 2010.

"The Shadow", "The Promise" and "How to Do It Wrong" are taken from *Three Men Talking About Things They Kinda Know About*, A Spoken Word Play written by Colm Keegan, Kalle Ryan and Stephen James Smith.

The Depaul Series were written in conjunction with service users at the Back Lane and Clancy hostels, both run by Depaul Ireland. The works were displayed as part of Depaul's 'Life's No Picnic on the Streets' Exhibition 2011.

Thanks to Ma and Da, Eileen Casey, Dermot Bolger, Bob Byrne, Paddy Kennedy, Stephen Kennedy, John Murphy, Dave Lordan, Brian Kirk, Tony Higgins, Stephen James Smith, Kalle Ryan, Shirley Chance, Louise Phillips. All at Lucan Writers, Eblana Writers, South County Dublin Libraries, Nuala and all at Arena, Ria and all at Depaul.

Very special thanks to Genevieve, for making it all possible.

Contents

HOME

IN-ROADS

LAST ESTATE

Stony, Grey, Soiled

After Kavanagh

Ballymun you rock hard bitch
My childhood love you thieved.
Your harsh nature quarried my passion.
You carved me from barren streets.

You concreted the feet of my boyhood
And twisted my stride to a stumble.
Your sprawl corrupted my naïve tongue,
Indian-inking my guttural mumble.

You preached from the trough of the scrounger,
The heaving, life-strangling trough.
Your mantra stained, your culture stunted,
You kept diamonds dull, in the rough.

You screamed 'cross piss-stained balconies
The wail of the deserted brood.
You stewed my clothes in smoke and booze
You reared me on stale food.

Your silhouette sours my vision
Of beauty, love and truth.
Ballymun, you barren whore
You spoiled the stock of my youth.

Not for me golden views of mothers
As poverty free young hens,
So I vow to stab at your crusted back
And embrace the poisoned pen

That scars these loveless verses
And curses the tarmac where
The first clean flight of my fury
Got caught in this poet's prayer.

Ceannt, McDermott, Balbutcher, Shangan,
Wherever I run I see
The stony grey rubble of Ballymun
Rebuilt as dark towers in me.

GREEN BELT

Hazelnuts

The hazel grove.
A schoolboy's paradise.
Five minutes in a car.
Forever using eight year old legs
through cornfields.
Concrete? What concrete?
Heaven on earth
to me at eight.
Trickling water
fluttering leaves
the smell of moss and
rotting trees
turning to muck.
And hazelnuts.
Real
bleeding
hazelnuts.
Not from a shop
from a tree.
From God to me.
From then on in
and even now I see –
the whole world is in my grasp.
The whole world belongs to me (for sharing).
Nothing can stop me eating hazelnuts.
Beautiful
brown
shiny like eggs.
I filled a plastic bag –
blue it was.
I carried them
all the way home.
I only ate a few.
But I'll never forget

those trees I climbed
the hills I rolled down
the hazelnuts
the sunlight
the smiles.

Fire God

Quick bright hot merciless.
Set loose by neglect
and ignorant too.
After everything important
it ransacked my house.
Ate my toys my posters
my clothes my shoes.
In its wake it left me
a charcoal castle.
Firemen not seeing me
puddles in the hall.
And in the cubby hole
my plastic
rocking horse.
Still standing
not melted
unbeaten
still yellow 'n all.

What a man

She'd come back from across the Liffey
with her two uprooted sons.
A husk of a husband left behind
'cause my 'uncle' was the One.

Streetlight licked
the black bags she carted
like stars in the sky
to my upturned eyes.

The plastic bursting open
like my heart with her return
and her heart with love for him.

I ran home and told –
my uncle just nodded
told Pauline (the other woman)
he'd be back in a minute
put on his slip-ons
and walked out the back door
to disappear over the wall.

People's lives around his absence
like empty beer cans.

What a man.

Taxidermy

There was a mongoose
and there was a cobra.
The mongoose was taking
the cobra on no problem.
You could watch this fight
this scrap on pause.
The cobra striking.
The mongoose coiling
in a glass case
in a pub in the mountains
that also had Wonder Boy
the best arcade game
you could ever play at the time
before drink driving
became socially unacceptable.
When your step-da would return
with the bumper gone
after a tree jumped out at him
and your uncle would just
shake his head
like it was a sitcom.
You would have loved that mongoose
almost as much as you loved your Da
who wasn't around
who was unemployed
but punched a clock one time and said,
"Tell your Ma that's when I dropped you off."
There were lots of pubs in the mountains.
The adults always talked
as if everybody was really friendly
and not drunk.
The mongoose in the glass –
That was your Ma.
The cobra was your Step-Da.

Fridays

For Damien

You're wearing your
snorkel jacket
because it's cold
and you have to go
across that road
the childhood road
you always picture
in the 'quick quick
call John an ambulance' joke.

Skippy's on but
you're missing it
your Ma had her reasons
but you're blaming her.
She wouldn't even bother
to walk you over.

In the time before phones
you stand and wait
in the pre-arranged
pick-up zone
the empty space
the airlock between
the outside world
and the next life
inside the pub
for your Da
who'll never turn up.

Christmas!

Christmas!
Yay!
Where's the toys?
In the bedroom!
No way!
A whole
Bleedin'
Action man!
Yeah!
A Space Ranger!
With a space-ship!
With a real rubber suit!

Christmas!
Glow in the Dark!
Quick!
The lights
hmm green goo glow
is satisfactory.
Rubber suit and space-ship
needs testing obviously
in water!

Christmas!
At the end of your bed Damo!
A whole Go-Kart. No way!
What time is it.
Five?
Woh.
Let's not wake Ma just yet
I'm gonna fill the bath.

Christmas!
Neearrown!
Die space aliens die!
Kersplosh.
Waters goin' cold.
Hmm.
Right then Damo.
Let's see how
this Go-kart
handles them stairs.

Woh!
Look at it go!
Glad we didn't sit in it.
Fuck!
Here comes Ma!
We'll get away with it though.

Christmas!

Miss Piggy

Miss Piggy he called her.
Harder than any
punch he ever threw.
It was all okay at first.
My Ma and his
woman in the pub.
Then he walked in
and even at my age
I felt guilty.

All the way home
he said it from behind
"Better get home Miss Piggy"
"Hurry up Miss Piggy"
over and over.
She was snivelling and choking.
The words worked her
like a leash.

I felt marked somehow.

From sights like this
perhaps all men are grown,
nice men
like doctors and painters
from seeds sown on the day
that they suffer
the first strokes
of a Master.

Blown Backwards

It was sunny before the hailstones
but now she's soaked to the skin.
Maybe they'll frown more today
when she buys a naggin this early
with her skinny toddler in tow.

She's hoping the booze will help
to erase the jarring memory
of last night's rain of punches
battering her howling face
after coming home late again.

Her son staring at the swirling sky
dumbstruck by the sight of a crow
being blown backwards
tugs at his mother's coat
hoping she'll share his wonder.

From behind her smoke-stained teeth
her vodka-starved tongue answers
like some tormented circus animal
taking any opportunity to snap.

With the icy curses spattering
and the hail that stings his face
something else crystallises
as he keeps his eyes to the sky
where the crow struggles on.

Glowing Embers

A gang of us there was
Martin the funniest one
Heno red haired and brazen
Jako and Dunner metallers both
and me blond and baby faced.

And then the girls
Loreta with the knockers
Tanya chewing gum
and Sharon
the girl next door
with those eyes
I got lost in.

That summer we lied
to our oul' ones
*"I sway'er I'm stayin in Heno's.
Ask his ma if you want,"*
before meeting in the evening
alive to adventure.

First we hid in a coalshed
swapping thoughts
in the shadows
slagging each other
fighting over fag ends.
Small fires burning.

Then we wandered
through Jobstown.
Ending up in the muckhills
where the wilderness
cradled us like bandits
huddled under the stars.

Today's streets are colder
without their smiles
under the orange streetlights.
The way we warmed to each other
like glowing embers
keeping each other alight.

SUB-URBAN

No Go Area

They don't build statues
for the likes of us.
No circle of angels
at our feet on the street
no mounted bust.

We don't make policy
shape the nation
or battle
on behalf
of the downtrodden.
We battle our selves.

Our fathers and mothers
our junkie brothers.
We fell them with baseball bats
play tit for tat with our 'neighbours'.

The worst of the world
falls on us like snow.
All our potential kept
in the dark unknown.

Like seeds on fallow soil
along the green belt
our homes are thrown up.
People left too close
to each other's self disgust.
Left together to stew
in mutual hatred.
Lives truncated by too much
fags and booze and bingo.

And the lingo
a law unto itself.
The code of the street
a pathetic bleat of sheep
so beaten into their pens
they think to aspire means
to conspire with the local dealer.
Never-ending
disputes over patches.
Men
like dogs pissing
outside their doors.
Drugs
blood
two by fours
and concrete blocks on heads.

And all the ones who see
the flaws can do is run
like every other migrant
chasing that never setting sun
that just turns out to be disdain
like flames on their skin.

Once outside your difference
becomes obvious
dress up in a suit
you must be the accused.
Your accent the source of amusement
the story bud
no sirree boss
how's it goin' hoss?
Cliché of everybody's yesterday.

But the thing that never goes away
is that everybody spoke like this once.
We are what was before.

We are forevermore
the uncosmopolitan.
Unlike you we suck nothing in
no Abercrombie
no Dubes or Nike swoosh
no politics
no D4 Foxrock bollocks.
We suck nothing in.
We aren't fucking chameleons.
We stick it out.
The truth on us like freckles
like Indian ink on our skin.

"Burn It Smash It Kill It Trash It"

After graffiti on a Clondalkin wall

Dope smoking
coke and yoking
early school leaver.
Not your goody two shoes.
Not your golden retriever.
Not on no fasttrack.
No future.
Take it or leave it.
Fucks like you always do sure.

Looks around here and sees
nothing worth doing
but drinking and stealing
and breaking and using.
Sees blokes turning women
into doormats for abusing.
Women looking up
to being a man's source
of amusement.
Blokes who live for the weekend.
Girls who denounce their mothers.
Featureless caricatures.
Carbon copies of each other.

He wants to be like them.
That's what he'd rather be.

His best friend hung himself.
Threw himself out on the street.
Lay hanging from his windowsill
with his neck broke by his bedsheets.
Found by his own mother.
Page still up on Bebo.
Straightforward bloke.
You'd forget him
if you'd seen him.

He just took a look around
saying 'What's the fucking point?'
Needing something to fill the gap,
besides
another
fucking
joint.

Nothing was the answer
nothing was the roar that
burned his ears
broke his heart
so he locked his bedroom door
saying –

"That's it Planet Earth
goodnight and fuck you all.
Where's the song that I can hear
where's the meaning
where's the call?
I'm listening
can you hear me?"

But there was nothing there at all.

At night during the witching hour
he thinks of taking his friend's place
until rage boils up into the urge
to grab his best friend's face

and scream

"Take your slump you beautiful fuck.
Go get angry.
Shake things up.
Stick your despair up their fucking jacksie.
Go out and break something!
Go out and smash anything!"

Dope smoking
coke and yoking
early school leaver.
Not your goody two shoes.
Not your golden retriever.

Lovebomb

The boy is a plank smashed
into another boy's teeth.
The boy is ripped open
by street corners
broken beer-bottle bits
rage vented on his flesh.

The boy is a first kiss
in a piss-stained stairwell
the sun beaming in through slats.
The boy is running in a pack
to the top floor of the flats
and howling at seagulls.

The boy is all this
and a myriad of tiny
miracles and cataclysms
before five years of age.

The boy is lost
pushing out through the concentric
rings of the city's development.
Shedding skins and ideologies.
Never feeling at home.
Looking in on each new
housing estate of mind
with an outsider's bewilderment.
Always haunted by a desire
for roots and belonging until
the girl comes along
and immeasurable want
rings through his bones.

The boy is with the girl
on the edge of the city.
On a verge scorched by bonfires.
On a manhole with grass
like green flames
shooting out around it
before the concrete gives
way to the fields,
back roads and hedgerows.
Daisies and dandelions
greens and whites and yellows
of a hazy never-rained-on summer.

The girl is raven haired and blue eyed.
Bright and gorgeous and full of fight
crawling out from under
an ancient shadow of religion,
guilt and denial.
The girl is orphan's hoarse from crying
laundries and women in black
with wasting wombs spitting hate
instead of love and fear instead of hope.

The girl is history's river of vitriol
poured into her innocent mother
and regurgitated into the present.
The girl is the apex of an upside down
pyramid of hypocrisy and violence.
The girl is a divine refusal to curl up and die.

And they've both just finished a joint.

The boy has a token.
A single sweet in his pocket.
One pink love heart.
He's been holding on to it
since the three words stamped on it

set him alight as if his heart
were a Halloween sparkler
fighting the night with
everything he liked about the girl.
The way he's desperate to touch her neck
the way he wakes thinking of her laugh
the way she makes his insides feel
deep and dark like a windswept crater lake
when she's near him and
like a vacuum when she isn't.

The love heart is as heavy
as a planet in his palm.

The girl lies back.
She watches a vapour trail crossing
the blue bowl of the sky
from horizon to horizon.
It's reflected in her eyes.
Her tongue feels fat and
hash-dry in her mouth.

The boy's blood pulses in his ears.
He hears the rush of traffic
the swirl of water beneath
the manhole he's sitting on
and he knows
he knows –
everything.

Everything was leading up to this.

He passes the sweet
into the girl's unknowing hand.
She reads what it says,
turns her slowly closing eyes away.
Places the words between her lips.

Juices flow into her mouth.
She spins the disc between her teeth.
The boy's breath quickens.
The girl's tastebuds tingle.
The sweet fizzes.

And after a while
she turns back
catches the boy's eye.
He leans over and
the girl is kissed by the boy.

And from that kiss
two whole new
worlds explode.

One Kick

(for the Father)

One kick
one tiny flick
of his two year old's foot
and he was hooked.
No matter what the mother did
his chubby soccer mad
little kid would feel his love forever.

But he never saw a day like this.
When a broken mother's courtroom kiss
would be all his son would have
for the next ten years.
No sun filled summers
no glittering career.

Just tears and regret
for the man he bet up
and the way one flick
one drunk and deadly
too strong kick
can crush a skull.

Ode to the Coalman

i.m. Mick Murray

From the black and holy heart of Dublin city
your legend was born in whispers
flickering into life around the flames
that fired our knacker drinking
taking flight in drug brightened
ravers' eyes on dawn strolls home.

Tales told of the alarming way you'd frighten
huddled jack-the-lads appearing
like ol' Nick himself or the Candyman
taking their two litres of cider from
their shivering all-cops-are-bastards hands.

We heard stories of explosive power.
You throwing a swarm of culchie Gardai
off your leather-coated back
with a swing of one ape-like arm.

You escaping as they chased
in a fleet of marauding shitvans
by leaping the too-high pointed fence
of Sundrive Park in a single bound.

"The size of him!" we heard.
*"The sound of him landing
would make your ears bleed."*

You smashed into our lives
like superhuman feet on concrete.

I saw you myself in the monsterflesh
one rainy morning on Wood Quay
towering like a berserker
screaming at the paperman and me
waving your caber-like staff
at the diamond kissed cars.
A wild black dog on a rope beside you barking.

You could be the stuff of Black Pitts
legend like Bang Bang with his key
and Johnny Fortycoats
from Clanbrassil Street.
Characters as big and bohemian
as the Liberties themselves.

But no. How could you be?
You're more like the city than they
for beneath the myth and the lie
hides the darker truth.

From the torment of your seventies youth
you lashed out and blinded a friend.
The spikes of your shattered pint glass
ate his face and tore out his left eye.
Why? The why is lost to time.

But not your return. No.
Not content with damage done.
Too insane, too dangerous to let a dead eye die
you traced your way back
to the townlands of that slaughtered friendship
two decades on when the blinded man
was dead in the ground from drink and loneliness.

With him only a few days gone
you planted your heavy booted feet
outside the twouptwodown
that mourned him
and with a cackling roar
you hurled a flaming bottle
though his front door
and left his Guiney's curtains
his vinyl records
his everything to burn.

Your legend lives on.

The Message

Weapon gripped
knuckles white.
Blood will be spilt
on this street tonight.
He has his brothers
his fellow men.
They face the enemy
one waves a machete.
Knees bent.
Teeth eating at themselves.

He grabs their leader
they tussle
he dishes out spite.
Scalp splinters
teeth chip
bone gleams
bright white bright white.
They wade through
each other
a mill of men.
All they have said
he makes them regret.
The message is sent.
Written on the ground in blood.
He is the winner.
Gets home.
Heats dinner in the microwave.

Eats.

Sleeps.

Dawn.

On stumble the police
to clean up and wonder.
Workmen pass
wither and shrivel
as they feel the stain
and ponder the pain.

The blood is soon gone
washed away.
The message remains.

Dealer's Buying Decking

Dealer's buying decking

      lays it down like tracks

over smackheads laid

      ten bodies deep

with needles in their backs

      he's going to put a pond in

piss in it when it's done

      he's planning a gazebo

from the bones of

      someone's son

he's bought up all the bouncers

      he almost owns the town

he wants to fuck your daughters

      he wants to break you down

his car has tinted windows

      so you cannot see his teeth

his acts are snowflake

      razor blades and

buzzsaws on your streets

    he wants to take your butterfly

crush it in his hand

    make you eat the broken wings

until you understand

    that his blanket

is your darkened streets

    his hero is your snake

his cock his only compass

    what he cannot have

he'll take

    his head is filled

with blood and war

    it rages in his head

TV has stabbed his eyes out

    his brain is turned to lead

his heart's a greedy vacuum

    he's only twenty four

his car is out there idling

    he's staring at your door.

Shut the Baby Up

Stab Stab Stab

Getting you back

Killing

                    You

Stabbing

                    You

Knife attack

Junkie

broken

history

    Junkie

        Broken

All cracked

Take it

                    Take it

Scum

                            Bag

The knife goes in

the knife goes in

the knife goes in

Shut the baby up

the baby up

I can't

My Pinned eyes

My Bared teeth

Soul blown to static

Grab the girlfriend

Get   the   girlfriend

Stickherintheback

Get

the

wallet

get

the

purse

Nearly at Blanch

Take it

take it

All the blood

      so black

Car skids

People running

Hear the baby crying

Taxi man

    bleeding out

Girlfriend crying

Shutthebabyupthebabyup

Rage multiplying

Dynamo in my
ribcage like my heart is
full of skeletons with bleeding
eyes rib-bones in flames

this is damnation

Shut the baby up the baby up Shut
the baby up the baby up
Shut the baby up
the baby up
Shut the baby up the baby up
the baby up the baby up
the baby

Murphy's Phone

People who fall down the stairs
ring Murphy's phone.
People whose kids died in custody
girls on the game, who were raped
but had Gardai laugh in there face
'cause like, Hello!

People who were hurt
people who want to complain
people who moan in pain
people who've been wronged so much
their souls are like black holes.

Murphy, the copper who sits
never answering the phone
was once a young naïve rookie.
Passionate.
He didn't see the machine
as he does now
as a cantankerous ship
a star destroyer
without a steering mechanism
and him on the deck
opening and closing
his silverminted mouth
and blowing in the wind
saying *"look between you and me
they'll get off with it."*

Years ago, before his beer belly
before his brain congealed
before his coarsening.
he would never be seen
preparing your file for the D.P.P.
by losing it down the back of a radiator.

But not now.
Now he never answers that fucking phone.
You never even get an engaged tone
or a "*your call is important to us*".
You just get the ringing sound
ringing and
ringing
and ringing
for help.

Help.

Most just put the receiver down
become infected
like Murphy himself.

But say you weren't content with that.
Say you went to see Murphy face to face.
You'd be asked to wait outside
like one of those awkward doctor's appointments
you might have two shiners
a busted lip
and a mouthy slice in one eyebrow
from a kick.

Mere coincidence.
The consequence of
say
a three to one
Nightlink main event
that would be nothing compared
to why you were there.
Trying to pull two lives from
a tear in time
that sucks at you still.

You'd find Murphy
polite and smart looking
in his beige chords and a white shirt
with a blood red pinstripe.
You might think
he looked like someone
you could actually like.

But when he opened his mouth
every word
would become
*"The only surviving systems
are self protecting systems."*

And before your eyes
Murphy would morph
into the man who holds his nose
driving through your estate.

And you'd never go back.

May you never have to
ring Murphy's phone.
It's a horrible thing.
It rings and
it rings
and it rings.

Memorial

'If poetry could truly tell it backwards, then it would.'
CAROL ANN DUFFY

They say in memory of you
there is a blessed bouquet tied
to the last in a row of lampposts
that shine their lights on
wasteground near your home.

The flowers go from wilted
to vibrant before being untied slowly
and taken down by your mother
who walks backwards into town.

Go back a few days more to her
and all your family gathering,
standing around you silently
in the field and watching.

You're removed from plastic.
Eyes closed, you're slid
into a drainage ditch, where

from dawn to when the cowslip
closes to midnight and beyond, heat
creeps from the grass into your body.

In the dark three men will come
with tools they use to pour
blood and bits into your stomach.

While you rise up and scream
they watch the muck and grass
leaving your three striped tracksuit.

They suck the pain and damage
from your bruises with their fists
and turn it into angry shouts
they swallow while their tools
are quietly hidden in their pockets.

Together you all run back in time,
past the lampposts into a garden,
the weeds all crooked and unkempt,
shrinking back from them before
they skip in through the back door,

returning to the shadows
of a house filled with your friends:
young good-looking boys and girls
music and a party starting
as soon as you step in.

Smog

We've got our 1990s clothes on.
Carpet jackets over
tracksuit bottoms and Kickers.
We listen to ten speakered monster radio
playing the Prodigy.

Our lungs are full of joint tokes.
Mouths gagged by damp scarves
cloaked in slag heap bituminous coal smoke.

We're hard
like the ever-ready teenage
cock in our cax.
And the pelt of our feet
on time stricken concrete.

We know the adrenalin buzz
of rearranging a face with a headbutt
the beaten boy's body gone limp in our grip.

This is what a gang can do
come over here and say that
I fucking dare you.

Our hearts oscillate
we are a glorious bloom
of vandalism.
The witching hour wakes us with wheelspins
stones raining on Shitvans and fire engines
bottles cartwheeling through the air.
Glass becomes shards beneath our fists.

The streets don't care so we don't care.

We're screaming it.

Outside
that's all you'll see.
But inside that we
lies me.
The geek
upstairs under the bed.

Reading.

HOME

"The Shadow", "The Promise" and "How to Do It Wrong" are taken from *Three Men Talking About Things They Kinda Know About,* A Spoken Word Play written by Colm Keegan, Kalle Ryan and Stephen James Smith.

The Shadow

if anyone asks I say
I was born in Ballymun
those cavernous towers of forlorn concrete
where human sounds bounce around
to swirl through the piss-stained balconies

but all tired clichés of urban bleakness aside
on a sunny day it was still amazing
to have a house up in the sky

I can remember being four years of age
peeping over the balcony
the gulls flying at the same eye level as me
the world below like a tapestry

and across the road
a rolling prairie of football fields
with the blocks of flats
like sentinels around it

that's where I had my first picnic
and with my Ma and Da watching me
I walked on grass
in my bare feet
for the first time

it was high summer
but the grass was cold
I can remember the fear of stepping onto it
and then the spring in it
the feeling of it tickling my soles
I'm getting tingles from my knees down
just thinking about it

I toddled back and forth
between the two of them

my father who
had a certain smell
a muskiness
that to me is synonymous with strength
and ambivalence
my mother was an all consuming
welcomeness
a nuzzle and a hug
if I lost my balance

I felt so at ease
crossing between them
not knowing that within a year
my father would be gone
off down the balcony
to become someone
only seen on weekends
like a movie

and then a memory
and then a shadow
that I'd later find in some old photo album
and think of as just some charismatic man
I didn't know

I broke my leg
soon after that barefoot walk
smashed it into the ground
my shin snapped like a kit-kat
I'm getting tingles from my knees down
just thinking about it

your original landscapes
they're what make or break you really
what you run to and what you run from
what you climb up on and what you fall off
the body learns when to flinch
when to strike out in self defence
the heart does too

The Promise

when I was seventeen
I fell in love with the dark haired
blue eyed girl of my dreams
right on the cusp
of the second summer of love
when the rave scene was still
innocent
carefree
peace love and unity

and during the biggest rave
Dublin had ever seen
we kissed in the strobes
and the laser beams

we became inseparable then
it had an inevitability to it
we went everywhere together
couldn't travel on a bus
without wrapping around
each other first
shared everything
headphones
joints
icecreams
cigarette butts

I used to draw her pictures
of a little raver flying up to the stars
a mutual friend had it tattooed on his arm
betcha he's proud of that now
I wrote her poems even
"show me any mountain to climb for you" I said
"show me any sea to swim
for you have ignited a fire in my heart
which no-one can ever dim"

once we got the Dart
out to Bray seafront
I remember her freaking out
and laughing
after I fucked her into the sea
stupid boyish thing to do
but funny

that evening we kissed
in the shadows of the promenade
my hands on her hips
salt on our lips
she whispered *"Colm's little pecks"*
as I kissed her cheeks
with the tide coming in
around our feet

and connecting it all
those ritual phone calls
that tug in the gut
from the dreaded engaged tone
or the flutter in my throat
at her evocative hello
spending hours talking
not caring what's being said
just loving the play in our voices
saying *"you hang up
no you hang up instead"*

and at the end of one July
my family went away for the week
I sneaked her out to the house
we shared our bodies like secrets

two years we were like that
free to enjoy each other's company

until the news nobody is ready for
a pregnancy
and nine months later
in the delivery ward
she handed me my daughter
I shaded just opened blue eyes
from the fluorescent lights
and I promised
I'd never leave

How to Do It Wrong

in the absence of a template for a father
become haunted by the ideal of a man
business suit
briefcase
coming home from work
the wife smiling at the door with the baby
and every time your life isn't like that
bring the real thing closer to collapsing

move in to a fully furnished apartment
laid out for a grown up couple
as the direction of your life changes
watch old friends slipping away
react to this like the teenagers you are
have what ought to be normal fights
amplified by feeling robbed of the choice
to be together or not

paper over the cracks
slide so far away from who you were before
until it feels like there's no way back
embrace the life mapped out for you both
as if stepping into a strait–jacket

want something more of life
while nothing ever changes
cave into the cliché
of the too much too young parent
stay stuck in that outmoded mould
right into your twenties
move house
have another baby

instead of spending more time with the girl
you're supposed to love
play with yourself
get addicted to hobbies
get a guitar and get okay at it
get a games console and live on it
disappear into the internet

in the mix of bread-winning and parenting
lose any sense of the original attraction
bury the feeling that things aren't right
retreat into a hard won selfishness
keep doing it like this
until the whole relationship
is like a kiss where
you keep banging teeth

conceal any vulnerability
invest less and less
in a game of diminishing returns
stop saying I love you at the end of phone calls
sleep on so many arguments
that your heart closes in
forget the value of a genuine apology
get used to going for days
then weeks without talking
learn not to need each other
feel more and more alone together

then stop
realise what's been missing
throw everything at it to make it work
and when that doesn't work
watch as things get worse
and worse
and let go
and in letting go

of the ideal
let go of it all
and fall

fall deeper and deeper into the black hole of yourself
becoming a pub crawling booze gorging loner in the rain
missing the last bus home chasing too many tails
through the closing time zone as you go off the rails
let your loneliness ring out like a smacked tuning fork
like a beacon as you lie and spiral out of control
hurt people drink harder
never once make amends
drown the guilt with more drink
repeat again and again
keep going get lost
fuck it all lose friends
fall apart completely
get told you're depressed
deny it
wonder if you're dying
refuse to accept how lost you've become

go numb
until the only option is to go
walk
realising you'd been going all along
into all you never wanted to be
the broken promise
the absent father
the shadow vanishing down the road

your mistakes following on behind you
like ragged ends on a tattered coat
a small part of you knowing
if you could do it all again

you'd do it better

Creature Falls

Twilight walk – burgeoning forest
Ivy rampaging over mossy ground.
My dog tearing roots from the undergrowth.
Something crashing through a hedge
makes me look around.

Creature falls towards me doing up his fly.

Raw meat wrapped in paper tucked under one arm.
Showing teeth he stares me down
through these bloodshot eyes
smirking once he realises I'll do him no harm.

Hawking he spits phlegm through a b-movie sneer
scrapes shit off one sole – rubs vomit from his jeans.
Takes a can of lager from his jacket and swigs
wiping dribbles from his unshaven jaw with his sleeve.

I know you, he says
I just shake my head
saying nah
you've me mixed up
with somebody else.

No.

Years ago, he says
*I watched you screwing some girl
on an ESB box at the back of the Mill.*

He swigs again.
Offers me the can.
Pointing it at me
like a gun in his hand.

I have no answer.

I know your sort, he says
with your wilted walk
talking like a tame man
with your neutered dog.
But still here you are
on the wrong side of the park
'cause you can take out the boy
but not the man from the dark.

I asked,
who are you to talk to me like that?

I'm your only Man, he Said
the Devil
the nick
the peace taken
missing tooth in the smile of the soul

Pimp
Ravisher
Bodice-ripper
Rake
Grasper of all the slapped chattels
of history noir and cowboy movies

Webcam jockey through the
united states of aimlessness
Happy-slapper of gullible faces
Exploiter of weakness
Fanner of debauched tails
Crawling forever backwards
into the holy womb of motherhood

The anti-hero
The dissipating waif
The masterpiece

of manipulative genius
The Lonesome Cowboy
naked-shieldless
protected
by an infinitely erected weapon

I am the capstone dreamt
onto a pyramid of
cavorting Sapphic women
doing your bidding
as they shrink from
your oh so mighty wrath

I am the wish
that they'd whittle
themselves away to
nothing but labia for you

Every time
the scent of a woman hits
the back of your throat

I'm snaking round
your frame like smoke
Whispering into your shell-like
Scaring the shivering witches
who see your aura
Flaring the nostrils of women
who know the cloak
of ever attracting blackness
bringing spit into the mouths of all
those rabid Pavlovian bitches

for whom damage forever swishes

around their stiletto
wearing pins like mist

I am Machismo

The shark fin
steering all into their bedroom
to fuck them into oblivion
to brand their arse
with palm-prints
to scar their hearts with
the lamb soft lick
of Casanova's kiss
the hand-made
hanger whip
of Iceberg Slim

I am the truth

You were born for this

Spent,
he took a breath.

Finished? I ventured.

Never,
he said.

So I picked up a rock
and smashed it into his skull
and when he fell
I did it again

and again

and again

I left him where he lay.

I pray that he's dead.

Stay Clear

It's late.
I'm staring at
a picture of my kids.
My two tomorrows in a frame.
They're looking at a sunrise.
Their sky is clear and golden.

Outside I hear the whip of blades
and a searchlight cuts the night.
Somewhere outside a man runs
jumping over back garden walls
like I did as a child when
breaking boundaries was fun.
But that man's having no fun
stooping in the shadows
imprisoned in infra red
running from some broken law.
Broken himself in a way.

All white in the spotlight.
A dead man
some would like to say.
Some might say there's
something wrong with me.
The way I root for him
the way I celebrate
when he makes it home
maybe crosses himself
in gratitude for tomorrow.

When his children's skies
stay clear and what shines
on him in the morning
doesn't chase him like a dog.

Coats

My daughter lost her temper
and swung her little white coat at me
making me laugh.
You should have seen her face
when it slipped from her arms
and took to the air.

I caught it for her.
But for a heartbeat
it was as if she thought
it might keep going
fluttering away from the playground
and over the Wicklow mountains
escaping to the sea and the sunset.

It might've met my jacket out there.
My little black jacket.
Size 3-4 with the gold
Benson and Hedges logo.
The one I took from the wardrobe
and slept in one night.
I used to live in it
and chew the collar.
I loved how the fabric felt in my mouth.

Until that day on O'Connell bridge
when I was sat beside it
the wind was raging
and whipped it from me
flung it into somersaults over the Liffey
where it landed gently on the oily water
and floated away.

Street Surfer

for Rebecca

She's an eight year old
street surfer.
She's real cool
in her little skinny jeans
bright eyes so blue
and her pink retro runners.

It gets you.

You'd know what I meant
if you saw the way she moves
through the park.
All clumsy and foolish
but ruling this planet.

Once in our house
she was laying on the ground
bent backwards over a beach ball
like Atlas upside down
but 50 miles away from tall
eating chocolate
(she manages to eat real loud
and never shut the fuck up at all).
I was waiting for her to fall.
"*We're all just a story
God writes every day*," she said.
I still don't know how
that got into her head.

She never fell.

She was born in November
which means she was
conceived in spring.
My little blue-eyed
pink-shoed skating thing.

And its spring now
and on she goes
skating on a yoke some
doped up hippy invented
to surf on land.
The daffodils
all around her nodding
in time with her hands
as she balances.
The lightness
in them and in her
moving in me like a sea.

French Toast (a recipe)

for Eileen Casey

For best results
watch Kramer vs. Kramer
at eight years of age or so
with your own parents already split.

When Dustin Hoffman
burns everything
and it ends in tears
feel sad for them both
and also for yourself.

Leave the memory to steep.
Throw in your first kiss.
That tickle of grass
on the soles of your childhood feet.

Let it sit.

Don't even know it's there.

Have French toast and maple syrup
with an aspiring friend.
Woody surroundings
fresh air.
But don't bake any connections.

Take the recipe home.
Hardly recognise its weight.

Leave the memory in the dark.

For the next few years
cook French toast
over and over.
Add the humble trials and traumas
of your budding family's life.

Replace maple syrup with sugar.
You're the only one
who really likes it anyway.

Let the family blend and mature.
Buy a trampoline.
Lose buddies
build firm friendships
keep buying a bigger car.

Fall in and out of love
with your partner and yourself
– repeat.

For best results
search your life for meaning
sometimes finding none.
Scatter old selves like used crusts
through the past.
Pepper your life with mistakes.
Accumulate some small
kernels of truth.
You'll need them over
and over as you go.

Preferably
your middle daughter
should shake you awake
on a Sunday morning
when you're hung-over
or just can't deal with getting up.

Hear her pleas for French toast
know what they actually are.
Stand up straight
slide on your slippers
stumble blinking into the kitchen

to guzzle orange juice
while standing over the pan.

Smile when your three-year-old
climbs up on the counter.
For once let her use
the whisk to beat the eggs.

Listen to your thirteen year old
come out of her room
like clockwork.
She knows what's cooking.

Dish it up.

Finally
watch the children
flit in and out of the kitchen
to bounce on the trampoline
in the sunshine.

Sit with a cup of tea
and your favourite book
on the history of the world.
One with maps
whose borders ebb and flow
over the ages like the tides
and be mindful of
how meaningless
all of that is.

Do all these things just so
and deep down inside
something dings.

IN-ROADS

Ireland Is

for Kalle Ryan

Ireland is so far gone from
Joyce's Dublin
but still fuelled by 'The Dead' and snow.
Upon quickly snorted cocaine breath we go.

Ireland is a badly bred, famine
stricken, flea bitten jalopy
of a Piebald horse galloping
down O'Connell Street.

Ireland is Cúchulainn with a hurley
gurning off of his head on Creatine
punching the face off the referee
before sticking him in the car boot
with sectarianism, and the disappeared.

Ireland is Tír Na nÓg;
Oisín saying Doh!
when his saddle broke.
Vikings raving on Wood Quay hill.
Monks driving Hum-Vees
through round towers they built.
St Patrick standing
with his fire on the mound
saying *"Honestly now*
that money was just resting in my account."

Ireland is English whether it likes it or not.
Laughing at Newswipe or Mock the Week
gorging on M&S food
ruining it's new Debenham's top.

Ireland is a Glock
pointed at someone's son
or a Christian brother
or it's own mother because
she won't move into the nursing home.

Ireland is a copper who looks like
Brendan Gleeson in 'Into the West' (in a chopper)
who'll put heroin in your hand and say
'Grand so thanks for the fingerprints
don't let the coffin door hit you on the way out
after you hang yourself with your shoelaces.'

Ireland is a teen-brained
new-age lapdancer
getting drunk.
Getting chlamydia of the soul
from too much unprotected
Facebooking down the boreens of
a ghost estate searching for Foxrock.

Ireland is veins butter fat
with broadband and self hatred.
Caught in the loop of a money shot lasso.
A faux-hawked, pentecostal, iconoclast, yahoo.
A liar in flames, in denial.
In the X Factor final of bullshit.
Gerry Adam's kissed by Barbra Streisand.
Bertie Ahern on screen crying.
Suicide, alcoholics, junkies, gunmen.
Dying and dying and dying.

And it's all so fucking electrifying
because we're fumbling blind.
We've no idea what we're doing
no idea where we're going
and we're almost there.

The Wind of the Spin

The two cars spun around
in front of me as if tied to the spire
of the church they passed
like kids swinging on a maypole
after smashing into each other.
Starting a song and dance and
crash of glass and steel that
made me think of cash registers or
coins falling from a bag burst open.

The unwholesome sound
was music in my ears.
I could almost hear this hum.
This low near silent thrum
of violence happening
a million times all over the world.

The symphony of accidents.
Airbags and shoulder
sockets popping.
Cars and people tossed around.
Scattered all across the earth
like runes or dice
along with those
sprinkles of ice or
some thrown down rain or
a patch of grass that
might speed or slow
the whipcrack
of an instant.

To make one car hit the front
instead of the back
so that one car spins
this way
not that.

So that me and all the other people
standing nearby feel
nothing but the wind
of the spin on our faces
like a kiss.

We all bear witness as
two men stumble out of
the wreckage to stare at
each other in disbelief.
Constellations of broken glass
beneath their feet.

Nobody wanting to dole out blame.
Nobody second guessing
the near miss.

Are you alright?
Are you alright?
they say.
While trying to reason this.
How close we came.

A Christmas Wish

In the longest evening
    Before the shortest day

When the sun is faded
    Along Grand Canal way

And the dew lingers deadly
    And the waters are still

And our breath cool clouds
    In the dead winter chill

Let a Christmas wish whirl
    Through the heavenless air

Let it find Kavanagh's statue
    And settle down there

Let it linger 'til darkness
    And when running Dublin sleeps

Let it raise the poet up
    From his cold bronze seat

Let the greeny avatar
    Walk our amber-lit streets

Let him enter Temple Bar
    Like a magnet to the people

Let him round up the hit-men
The whores and the mugged
The buskers
The barmaids
The loved and the drugged

Let him be a pied piper
    A tambourine man

Let him reel through the suburbs
    With the crowd behind dancing

Let him rob high-def houses
    Of their chilling girls and boys

Let him lead us in our thousands
    To the naked countryside

Let us follow him northward
    To the bend in the Boyne

Where the green fertile fields
    Are starlit and supine

Let us take to the 'grange
    Bundle into the mound

Let the earth be our coffin
    Let him follow us down

Let him block out the air
    With a giant spiralled stone

Let the cold from the granite
    Slither into our bones

In the womb of that tomb
    Let us taste the abyss

Let Kavanagh abandon us
    To the dark nothingness

And the dawn shining wonder

Through a small enough chink
Through a roofbox revealed
As the sun finds dominion
Let us enter the morning
Let the past fall away
Let us stand illuminated
In the New Year's Day

Nicola

I was the main man on
Championship Sprint.
King of the circuit
no-one could beat me.

I knew all its secrets.
How to dodge the oil slicks.
How to work the curves to get inside.

But girls?
They were a different game entirely.

It was there after two hours playing
without wasting one of my ten credits
that I felt you watching
over my shoulder.

You who'd wangled your way in
to the 'Bru', a boys' only youth club
to whisper in my ear,
'You're brilliant at that game'.

Eyes on the screen
I tried to ignore you but
you wouldn't leave me alone.

Saying all your friends had left,
you asked me to walk you home.
I'd no idea what was going on.
Typical bloke.

We walked the maze of Crumlin streets
from St Agnes down to Leighlin green
bumping shoulders on Armagh Road.

Joke fighting we passed the take-away.
And outside the slightly opened school gates
you kept delaying
I remember saying
'What the fuck are you waiting for?'

All became clear at your front door.
You threw your arms around me and we kissed.
We held each other tight for seven years.

Written with John Devlin (Depaul Service User)

Cheek Cheek Chin and Nose

It was short
the way you spoke
you up on a pillar
me sitting down low.
The flow
of your words clipped
as you shot a rhyme
after a passing ambulance.

"Cheek cheek chin and nose," you said.
"Hope I never go in those.
If I do I will go –
Cheek cheek chin and nose."

And shorter still
was the distance
between your life and mine.
You got closer
than I would have liked
when you were furthest away
at your lowest ebb
caught in a web
of drugs and tricks.
And me in love with you
all along
with your voice
the song of it.
That's the long and the short of it.

You probably had a fit that night
when bad gear fell on the city
like bad weather
and wherever they found you
some poxy squat
or whatever
with rat poison in your veins.

It was a million miles away
from all the things
you could have been.
No white wedding for you
no babies on your knee.
Your two brothers left behind
you being the only girl.

The only girl.

Sometimes I think of Dublin
like a huge dirt ridden blanket –
moth eaten
holy
like something
shrouding a homeless man
something he tries to
smooth and smooth
something he thinks
can keep him warmer
but it never can.

Your ma –
she used to pray.
You'd be out
banging up or
who knows what
and she'd be at home
saying the rosary.
Watching the clock
ticking on your life.

And the closer you got
to your midnight
the further you were from me.

And I never said I liked you.
If I had said
maybe.

In my head
you wander round.
Stir up the dust.

I still remember that time
on the bus going
from Crumlin into town
and you appeared before me.
There were others around
but they're forgotten.
You're remembered
like a myth.

The way the sun shone
round your head.
You'd dyed your hair.
I just sat there.
You were chewing gum
your mouth gamming on
wearing a Levi's denim shirt
with the top button undone.
So close
we could have kissed.

Little did I know
by then your heart
was already lost.
The drugs had won.

Later
someone told me
that you were
only riddled

like
with the virus.
Like
a body full of bullet holes.

That's how he saw you.

But not me.

I'll always see you
on that bus.
The two of us
trundling into town.
Everything else crumbling
falling down all round.
And that shine in your face
some magic glow
some sickness
some song
that was the last rays
of your waning soul.

Rosemary

"Cheek cheek chin and nose," you said.
"Hope I never go in those.
If I do I will go –
Cheek cheek chin and nose."

Dear Dealer

Don't get me wrong:
I've had nice times with blokes like you.
Been in the company of some real nice joes.
Young bucks with bright clothes
dudes
buds and bros
who brighten a room with their presence.

But it is endlessly depressing
when you lean in close like that
and say *"Listen – If you're stuck,*
I'll hook you up:
I've Coke or blow,
just so you know."
And the way you wink,
not realising what I'm thinking.

Are you stupid or what?
Have you simply forgotten
all those other scurrying specimens?
Yeah sure
you'll be different.
You're going to make it:
you'll avoid the rats on the run
all the psychos with guns.

And if you do survive
you'll end up just like all the rest.
Making the common man's
worst nightmare
your twisted best.

As you develop a blindspot
for the children watching
when you shoot men in the head.
All hopscotch stopped dead
by some bro or Daddy's blood
spraying a short spattering rain
that burns like acid
into their childhoods.

But no
not you
hands open you plead.
You're one of the nice dealers,
you'll just take what you need
and have nothing to do
with the bodies piling up in newspapers.
Brains exposed to the air
a heaving mess of black thoughts and goo
to be tiptoed around
and waded through.

Not just by me
but by every other poor shmoe
who has to live in this coliseum
that your greedy claws
have the gall
to maul and shape
from the muck on
our once clean streets.

So please excuse me
if for the sake of my dignity
I will keep you away from me
and in my mind paint you black
as I smile with quiet tact
and count the targets
on your back as you leave.

Warpaint

1

Going through the steel doors in the Anarchists Ward
getting patted down with all those buzzers going off
reminds me of London where I went to dodge a warrant.
I wrecked a street of cars in a Vauxhaul Rekord
crashed into them all and tore the wing mirrors off
locked the wheel and spun to get the other side as well
with alarms screaming out and the houselights coming on.

2

Three months out and on me way back in
with a roll of charge sheets longer than me last stint.
Got stopped at the shop door with Jean Paul Gaultier perfume
seven cans of Bud packed in me clothes like armour.
They said we know it was you we have it here on camera
so I shotgunned a can and smashed it into the keyboard
saying there's your evidence now.

Security came down on me from all directions
a Russian guard jumped on me and broke me jaw.
I took out me works and stuck it in his face
he's lucky I left me bowie-knife in me hiding place.
Spent ages in hospital with me gob wired up
but I'm getting a claim out of it things are looking up.

Written with Anonymous Depaul Service User

Sycamore Seeds

Everything is inspired by nature.
They say that even the blades
of the helicopter came from
the seed of the sycamore tree
and one day the spark
that set Da Vinci's mind alight
set fire to mine.
Instead of flinging one into the air
while walking alone in the street
I tugged two handfuls from the tree.
Got home and told my boys
I wouldn't be a minute.
Crept up to the bedroom
to catch my two sons by surprise
as they played in our garden below.
I stuck my hands out the window.
Set the whole fleet free on the breeze
to spin around and flutter down
and fall like confetti at their feet.

There's pain in the memory.
But I see the joy in their eyes
the smiles on their faces
upturned in awe.
And love it all the same.

Written with Greg Davidson (Depaul Service User)

97

The Crackle

for Stephen Kennedy

There's a party full of 'Fat-Frogs'
and coke all over the table.
There's a man out by the Liffey
getting out while he's able.
There's a fight starting somewhere
a fellah getting stabbed.
There's a car doing hand-brakers
two girls jumping a cab.

There's twitchy bouncer hacks
keeping an eye on the door.
That poor lad in the jacks stuck
cleaning puke off the floor.
The country's getting locked.
There's nobody to care.
There's a slut going down
and there's danger in the air.

There's men drowned in money
girls who'll never bend.
There's a beggar whispering 'honey'
but that's nothing down his end.
There's the gentle sound of heartbeats.
There's alleys full of death.
There's a man after your brother.
There's a lightness to your breath.

All these people hanging around
everybody acting cool
and the night-times fucking freezing
but don't let that fool you.

There's a crackle to the city.
There's a steam of dreams that rises
and it gets behind your eyeballs
and it kind of compromises
the concrete
the shell
all the bits that sing *'to hell with it.'*
There's another bit
a hoping bit
that screams out

make a difference.

The city's
electricity.
It shines on us.
We're sparkling!

And love it man
'cause further out
there's nothing

only darkness.

LAST ESTATE

The Last Dry Friday

for Dave Lordan

Scatterbrained from something
in the air resonating
in a way that tugs at my attention.
Like tide at an anemone.
I park the car.

Through an archway beneath a railroad bridge
I am surprised to discover a darkened beach.
Feeling the forever pull of water
I step in.

My ears devour the crunch of gravel.
My pulled up hood
gives me that head-phoned in feeling.

In the starry sky
I see our galaxy cut
sharply by a belt of black
scudding the horizon.

The waves steam and churn
in the sodium glow from
astro-turf pitches nearby
and beyond that light
a stillness building.

While surfing once off the coast of Mayo
I was approached by a pod of dolphins.
First lone fins showing in the glimmering sea
and then one animal coming at me
in a wall of surging green
which rolled on underneath without breaking
while the others circled, never surfacing.

It was a beautiful thing
their disinterest in me.

That chimes now in the deep.
Rings in time with some internal quickening
as I stand on the nighttime beach
feeling the ocean's swell in my chest cavity.

All this ebb and flow
I don't know why I was born
why define ourselves through suffering
the core of our stories
the reason for everything
what to run from
what to run for.
Something ringing
and then the answering.

Lightning.

The first flash whipped my mind
a spark in the corner of my eye.
The second I sought but caught too late.
The third lit up the horizon in a
purple pink and
yellow synaptic crack
darting across the sky
molecule by tortured molecule.

There was no sound.

The atmosphere was torn in two
I felt a new world being stepped into.
Another was left behind.

Sometimes you feel like the ripple
sometimes you feel like the stone.
Right then I felt like both.

Woman

When I lived in Knockmore
I remember a commotion
one Sunday evening
around the time
John Tracey won the silver
in the Olympics.

A boy didn't want his mother to leave
and grabbed the bumper of a car
that she was getting a lift in.
He wouldn't let go
not when the car
sped down the road
not when his legs went
from under him
not even when the tarmac
tore the skin from
his shins and knees.

When it comes to women
that's always how I feel.

Twisted Together

Even in the silence
that neither of
us will break
the truth lurks.
The ugliness
between us.
Those times
we screamed
and hurt each other.

All the lost stings
clipped wings
and failings
would break your heart.

So broken now
two twisting things
we work and
sweat together
kneading closeness
out of flesh
turning lies into
a beautiful truth
that floats
there for a moment
before it's gone.

Afterwards

Afterwards we sleep
you fall off first sometimes
and sometimes if I doze off instead
I wake with a fright from one
of those falling or dying dreams.
But one time I woke
and you were in the grip of
one of your own, shaking
arguing with some shadow
until your voice softened
and had a freedom, a lilt
that it never has when waking.

Your whispers swirled around me
and trickled down my spine
I felt transported, inside
the cathedral of your mind.
The shine of your secret words
warmed me like the glow
of dreamlight cascading
through a stained glass window.
I touched your cheek.
I kissed your forehead.
Outside the last bus
went rushing past our home.

Chalks

These coloured chalks
fell into my lap.
Fruit from a swaying bag
of a passerby.
So I use them
to plead and swear
upon the slabs
that you wear and tear upon
and smooth out with your feet.
"*Look at me!*" I write
"*I am beneath you like the pool
from a leaky radiator,
like the roots beneath the trees.*"

My knees don't feel
the cold housed in the concrete.
I gave up on heat.
Your street
is a barren whore to me
anyway.

I seek to plant nothing
but words.
And if the rain
washes them away
if no-one sees what I say
the chalk dust
at least
will brighten the dirt
trapped by my fingernails.

The Moon and the Fire

'Look, at, the, fucking, moon.'

RICHIE EGAN/JAPE

I felt
the colour blue.
The noise
I heard was silence.
From the horizon
the twinkling of the city
injected orange into my heart
at the speed of light.

Above me in the sky
the moon halved
the clouds cleared to reveal
that plough made of stars
like an arrow pointing
saying look
the moon for you.

The dog sat
when I said sit
and I stood there
looking up at it.
It's brightness
a cold breeze inside my skull.
I felt so very very alive right then.

I was beyond the earshot of the
street
but above me
(I was on a hill)
or beneath me
or behind me
I heard someone speaking.

The park was so dark
I could not see.
This disembodied voice
it frightened me.

I turned to leave
but distant lights still
whispered their silent song to me.

So I stopped and stared
at a plume of smoke
where the lights ended
becoming –
aspiring
to be a cloud.

To twinkle is not to shine
there's more play in it
like a straight line
with a wobble worked in
each streetlight
like a Venus.

Of you and I
I am the only witness
the dog couldn't care less
but the plume
was made by fire I think.

A plane blinked its descent
not a dive
more a floating down
or the ground
moving up to take it
as we take butterflies.

Right then I thought
it would be okay to die.

COLM KEEGAN has read and performed his poetry at various festivals, including the Flat Lakes Festival, Electric Picnic and the Festival of World Cultures. He was the All Ireland Slam Poetry Champion in 2010. He also writes short stories and screenplays and has been shortlisted four times for the Hennessy New Irish Writing Award for both poetry and fiction. In 2008 he was shortlisted for the International  Seán Ó Faoláin Short Story Competition. In 2011 he was nominated for the Absolut Fringe's 'Little Gem' Award for the play *Three Men Talking About Things They Kinda Know About* (co-written with Kalle Ryan and Stephen James Smith) which is touring 2012/2013. He is a poetry/arts reviewer and contributing poet for RTE Radio One's nightly arts show ARENA and co-founder of 'Nighthawks at the Cobalt'. He is co-founder and facilitator of Inklinks, a young writers' club in Clondalkin and teaches creative writing in secondary schools across Ireland. He maintains a popular blog and his poetry performances are widely viewed on YouTube. He is currently finishing his first novel.